DUNCE

DU

WAVE BOOKS SEATTLE AND NEW YORK

Published by Wave Books

www.wavepoetry.com

Copyright © 2019 by Mary Ruefle

Wave Books titles are distributed to the trade by

Consortium Book Sales and Distribution

Phone: 800-283-3572 / SAN 631-760X

Library of Congress Cataloging-in-Publication Data

Names: Ruefle, Mary, 1952– author.

Title: Dunce / Mary Ruefle.

Description: First edition. | Seattle : Wave Books, [2019]

Identifiers: LCCN 2019000628 | ISBN 9781940696850 (trade hardcover)

Classification: LCC PS3568.U36 A6 2019 | DDC 811/.54—dc23

LC record available at https://lccn.loc.gov/2019000628

Designed by Crisis

Printed in the United States of America

9 8 7 6 5 4 3 2

Wave Books 078

Last night as I lay sleeping I dreamt

O, marvelous error—
That there was a beehive here inside my heart

And the golden bees were making white combs
And sweet honey from all my failures

ANTONIO MACHADO

DUNCE

APPLE IN WATER

I was swimming
with the taste of apple
in my mouth
a shred of appleskin
between my teeth I guess
It doesn't get any better than this
said the water
These are troubled times
said the shred
and the apple, the apple
wasn't really there,
only a lingering taste of it,
as if it were the last apple,
or an earlier one that had lasted,
either way it was silent
and I swam with the silence
in my mouth, listening to
the pretty crimson dot

and the great slipping glimpser,
not knowing whether I heard
a night of love
or a love of night,
such was the knowledge gained
during that long languid swim.

LONG WHITE CLOUD

How did the bare-bummed child crawling
on the beach in a pink sun-bonnet
learn how to walk by watching seagulls?

How did my mother decide to marry
my father by buffing her nails
then staring at her hands?

How did so many unpronounceable words
come into being? And how many more words
whose meanings are unclear or obscure?

Why do seagulls cry
while landbirds sing?

How did the Agitator of the Soul
become himself so violently agitated?

How could someone crying out
a cloud, a white cloud, a long white cloud
be naming a country?

A country is not a cloud
A cloud is not a country

Only the Agitator of the Soul
would have you believe it

Seabirds cry to be heard over the waves
Landbirds sing to let everyone know

A silky cornel of red osier
makes good kinnikinnick

My mother gave simple advice to all
Do not grow up to become a baby

And the baby stood
And the baby took a step
And then another
And the seagulls scattered

into a cloud, a white cloud,
a long white cloud
And the baby cried

To be heard over the land of the living

SOLOMON

Solomon didn't know what to do

Should he cut the baby in half
lengthwise or sidewise?

Each mum have an arm and a leg
or arms to one, legs to another?

Hearts can be broken in different ways

Think of him,
coming to the bath,
having to fill it
with his own spit

Not knowing what to do
until his work was done for him

And then he was off the hook,
a very large hook of the kind
they hang sides of beef from
in a refrigerated room

Afterwards, alone in his library
see how he wraps the broken spines
so carefully
each text will be called upon
to comfort another

DUNCE

I am always up for a bog, said Mary.
I, too, am always up for one, said I.
And so we put on our rubber boots.
I love being in rubber boots, said Mary,
and I said the same. The ground sprang
as we bogged, the bog wavered as we sprang,
orchids & mushrooms, mushrooms & orchids,
slender & pink, squat & brown.
And as the light fell the eyes of the fireflies
were all around, like Tinkerghosts.
There is in my house, she said, a stovelight
that never goes off. And in my car, I said,
there's a dashlight that never goes off.
What warning has no end and ends without warning?
She thought I didn't know!

THE GOOD FORTUNE OF MATERIAL EXISTENCE

Without bringing any more people
into the planning loop, I have decided
to have breakfast. I have made cautious
inquiries, and finally learned it is
Thursday. My attention sets out
in a cheerful mood on a memorable
expedition to the sink.
Oh blank and hopeless days!
Oh long sleepless nights!
They are forgotten now
as I turn on the cold clear
water of the stream.
All the rivers of the world
convene in me. They rush
over my hands, they enter

my mouth, they cover my face.
I am compelled to drink my own
tears, as you too will be
when you wake.

MARIA AND THE
HALLS OF PERISH

She loved dandelions
but hated the circus.
She wanted to know where eggs
came from, *really* came from,
where came the body of the body
of the body they came from.
And when her heart made
that sad little oboe note
she wanted to know where
the mind came from,
and was as answerless
as if she sat in the middle
of a beginningless river.
The beginning of the universe
reminded her of the time
the toy factory blew up

and she found a little clown
on the shore, and then another,
until she was determined to find
them all, the whole shebang,
though she never did, and night
fell over the ocean, and eye-popping
children of all ages slept in a sleep
brimming with irresistible attractions,
giving them a taste of what
awaited them when they woke,
though it was nothing compared
to the massive arrays of adulthood.

CRACKERBELL

I grew up

I became myself and
was haunted by it

and I loved to wander, utterly alone

listening to the sound of tears
striving to guess my own secret
and racking my imagination for
a dream

meanwhile,
everybody else knew my story
and there was not one of them
who would give me so much as
a bird dropping

so on I wandered
with arms and nitric-startled eyes,
nitpicking my way through the world
when the electrical current
that runs in all directions
deep beneath the earth
shook me

and at once I felt
there are so many years to fail
that to fail them all, one by one,
would give me a double life,
and I took it.

RESIN

I am going to die.
No such thought has ever occurred to me
since the beginning of my exclusive time
in air when I, having made up my mind,
first began to wrap it, slowly and continuously,
in strips of linen soaked in a special admixture
of rosewater, chicken fat, and pinecones
studded with cloves to stop them from dripping.
Nor is it likely I would ever have had such a thought
in the time required by me to finish the job,
if someone else had not first introduced the thought
into the process, thereby interrupting it,
however briefly. But who?

A LATE DENSE WORK

It is a beautiful day here in
Milford, NH
The warm of the sun feels good
on my back
The wild mountaintop flowers
are blooming in their wild glory
My face a thumbtack
in the earth

Do you want I should make
some rapt contemplation
descending into useless particulars?

I will be pressed also
when it's midnight
and snowing hard

MIDNIGHT EXPRESS

I smoked in profound silence,
wondering what would come next.
But nothing came next.
I am not what is called
a woman of imagination,
but I am not without a certain
psychological insight,
and I think I might have been
dwelling in the realm of gnomes
engaged in hoisting false signals
and misplacing switches
for the midnight express.
And now I feel a pause,
and now I jump over it
with sudden indescribable tenderness
as if actually bending over
a cradle, and now I feel
I am on my way: now I am

in my machine, the road rolling
beneath me, behind me,
in front of me, and it is no
imagination that I picture you
in your machine, or reading,
or washing your clothes,
though it is perhaps this one hour
you have chosen to make a list
of all the acts you are ashamed of,
or the ones that came to nothing
through no fault of your own,
so that you sit quietly
and in great silence,
like a gnome on a stump,
one of the older ones,
smoking a pipe filled with
bewilderment and regret.

GENERAL DIRECTION

I keep walking in the general direction.
Toward the horizon,
where things generally appear.
Tanks! Horses! Houses!
Another person, perhaps several.
I've come from sleep,
I'm well-rested but unfed.
A cistern would be nice.
The scent of little buns.
A soufflé with a flag on top.
How can anyone forget eggs?
They drop down in the body,
little troopers, and voilà—
legs, arms, electricity, running water.
The important things.
We all want them.
Everything else is icing,
which is supposedly bad for you,

so that once I ate a whole cake
by digging into the cave of it,
leaving the icing intact,
an igloo on a plate.
When the sun came up and hit it,
that was a disaster,
though a prophetic one.
Like a chandelier, I generally
stand apart from things
and with a cold eye.
But not today. Which brings
everyone up to the present.
I am walking in the general direction
of things. I plan to hang a handbill
announcing I was nothing
and shall be nothing again.
In the meantime, walking here
in the wind and rain,
apparently inspired,
I brace myself for a sortie.

EARTHLY FAILURE

The copier grew tired of copying,
made a terrible, sick sound
and died.

I told my friends the poem was
blurry because the copier wept
while reading it.

That poem ruined the world,
it made everyone shy.

Now I've ruined the poem,
there's nothing left
but a knight sticking his sword
in a snail.

TUNA AND A PLAY

Tonight we are having tuna and a play.
Earlier, I picked grasses with J.
Blue grass, pink grass, silver grass,
we each carried a bouquet.
I asked J if she was glad to be human—
J, are you glad to be a human?
but she couldn't say,
she walked through the grasses
for what seemed like a day,
I thought I saw her face turn gray
but it was no more than a moment
in a *very nice* day—
and tonight we are having *tuna* and a *play*.

SUDDENLY

It's like there's more oxygen
in the air or something
or 107 babies' faces have been enlarged
and are drifting across the sky
I also saw a leaf-blower
and all the dead leaves
looked like they were having fun
jumping around as if they were alive again
I think too of a certain recipe
that calls for eelgrass
which the scallops love to swim in
and on top of it all
a profound sense of nothingness
has come into play
so I tell everyone I was born
at sea among the meadow people
who never speak a word
that has not been repeated
over and over and over again
but still takes me completely
and by surprise

UNBEKNOWNST

Words have no thoughts
just as you have no
lice. And yet our mite
is often present, and never
seems by word or look
to disapprove of us.
Can the line be drawn
between paper
and all the brain-sickening
effluvia of reading?
Words you may find as you
read you may find as you read
you deepen them,
until tomorrow you can describe
the esslessness,
growing and winding about
in wild entanglement
within the little head—
ever where there is
no to be there!

DARK CORNER

I was cleaning an empty drawer
I wanted to put things in.
Not much there—
a dead fly, a dark penny,
a straight pin, dust
in the back corners.
As I crimped my fingers
to pick up the pin
a poem came to me.
That is, it appeared
word for word in my mind.
How did it get in the drawer?
How long had it waited?
Had *I* put it there,
in holding?
Did it belong to the *fly*?
Did he drop it from some lonely height
onto this playground of refuse,
his own death
come out of nowhere?

ATTENTION!

I hold the staff of the Great Sage
while he stands on the gorge-brink
gazing at mountains.
He is at this moment lost
in the mist of Existence,
while I am but his attendant—
Existence-Attendant!
The name of one who stands
like a stick, thinking of nothing.

LITTLE STREAM

My heart was bright and shining
like a lobster boiling in water.
And then I was just a child
eating the leftover snow.
I'd lost my mittens and my belly button
was as good as gone, meaning
I couldn't be born again, ever,
so I sat by a little stream
with my eyes closed.
I saw a woman carrying a child's coffin
on her head. I saw a rat so friendly
he shined my shoes with his tongue.
I saw my mother leave the room, saying
"Now I am going to go drink some vinegar."
I saw a surfer drink a wuthering wave
and go down gently into that good night.
I saw the daffodils praying together.
I saw a hummingbird cry out

for a comma between decades.

I saw the quick trimming the hair on their necks
and the wicks of their packaged feet.

I saw something small and in constant danger
of being blown away, like pepper.

I saw a monk set an umbrella on fire, for fun.

I saw an old man dwelling in a tiny fishing village
with a tangible vibrancy that was truly inspiring.

I saw a Venus flytrap eat a cheeseburger.

I saw my struggles were coming to a close.

I saw I would grow so old I would stop wondering
what life on Napa Rui was like, and forget
the first apple tree was in Turkey.

I had the constant feeling something of vital importance
had been lost sight of, was perhaps even gone.

It's hard to say hello to every atom.

I got to know protozoans, though.

It took three days for my umbilical cord
to swim past. At the end,
the tattered carnation of my navel
seemed most like me, so I threw it in
and at once my eyelids opened,
never to close again.

MEDITATION ON MY SKULL

There is the great lacuna.
No one knows what was there,
least of all me.
Some say a squirrel, a nut, and
a hole. Others suggest a wet cotton bag
pulsing with fireflies, ten yen apiece.
I doubt it. Though before I passed into
lacuna-land I did read a beautiful, sad
Japanese novel whose author killed himself
on my birthday. We could have met!
But yea there is a lacuna of the living
that keeps souls apart
in their own wicker cages.
The character for *think* also means
"be sad, yearn for, unable to forget."
As, in English, "I think of you"
has the shade of summer moonlight.
Also on my birthday I was born.

And on my deathday someone else
will be born (I think of them)
assuring us there is no lacuna
anywhere, even if my skull
passes beneath a cloud
on a summer's night.

NORTH WIND

Cannot say *I* as yet
but am beginning to get the idea
by putting the tip of my tongue
to the roof of my mouth.
Am exasperated when
do not succeed.
So much is missing
from the middle of the day!
Despite my best efforts
at individual enjoyment
know the north wind doth blow—
one day as yet
the roof will come off
and perishable below.

HAPPINESS

Summer late evening

my friend the sunset

to surprise me

took the most interesting streets

Late he was

Longer than ever before

LORRAINE

Once I had a plum tree.
It was small but sturdy
and every April I threw its petals
in the stream. They intoxicated everyone,
even the postman. Even the postman
knows I am more homesick than E.T.
and lonelier than my middle name.
I live with mice and bats where once
I had toy cars and paper airplanes.
Like a wild swan
with a blue shadow,
I no longer care what I say.
You no longer exist.
I try to remember my dream
but as soon as I turn on the shower
it's gone.

THE EVENTUALIST

Playing horsey in the field
I galloped toward the tremendous
growth of the rhubarb.
My job was to make Mother happy,
to follow the sound of the thrush
into the woods so the innocent leaves
could swallow my laughter.
Twice I made Mother happy,
once when I brought her an armload of rhubarb
and once when I bought her five pounds of talcum.
Eventually I read Trakl: *the mother moves through*
the lonely wood of this speechless grief.
Eventually I wrote *the powder of ill stars*
falls on us; eventually she found and read
my journals, which were full of such stuff
so she burned them.

ARE YOU TALKING ABOUT A FUNERAL?

One by one away they walked and went to their cars
and every one of them was crying . . .
it was as if they had spent the day exploring an island
only to be told afterwards it was the contours
of their own face . . .
or had been flipping pancakes with a needle
as Cervantes did, and failed more miserably than he . . .
they looked indeed as if they'd heard the falling snow
lecturing to the ground, or been told the stations of the cross
were nothing more than a stupid love affair
(*stay with me, what wondrous love, remember me, were you there?*)
Oh to the dark parking lot my friends,
I know of something you did not tell me,
though you wanted to, and I you,
as we trekked down from the volcano
in whose grassy green bowl we'd spent the day
chasing tiny white butterflies . . .

THE FRIEND

Once while walking
in the woods
my friend and I
found a bright
orange newt.
We looked at him
kindly, then went on.
Out of the night
my friend said
It pays to be
the friend of a newt.
And indeed it does,
in deed it does.
The years have
shown me that.

SENT TO THE MONK

Night falls
and the empty intimacy of the whole world
fills my heart to frothing.
The past has trudged to this one spot
with a flashlight in its mouth
and falls into the stream.
Ancient tears beneath the surface
rise and scatter like carp,
while an ivory hairpin floats away
like a loose tooth going back in time.

BATH TIME

With both ears I hear
the dainty popping
of bath bubbles—
and a light rain
falling on my mother's grave
comes back to me,
how it seemed
on that sans-everything day
to be the very pins
she carried in her mouth
to unlink a knotted chain for me
or affix a foreboding note,
for even a small child
knows the affliction
of language.

SEARCHLIGHT

Do you really want your holiday guests
looking at your current flooring?
That white hatchback is shaped
like a polar bear. What is the name
of the baby panda born last year
at the National Zoo? Who said
scatter lilies with open hands?
I wouldn't be caught dead in that outfit.
No woman no cry. Years ago
I ate dinner in Switzerland,
I looked down on the eyes
of my trout and remarked on those
bosoms where you cannot find the
perishable objects of the present life
followed by an interval of stillness:
the present moment
and the next hour and one minute
in the center of millions,
all pointing directly at your
heart, contracting.

I CANNOT BE
QUIET AN HOUR

I begin
to talk to violets.
Tears fall into my soup
and I drink them.
Sooner or later
everyone donates something.
I carry wood, stone, and
hay in my head.
The eyes of the violets
grow very wide.
At the end of the day
I reglue the broken foot
of the china shepherd
who has put up with me.
Next door, in the house
of the clock-repairer,

a hundred clocks tick
at once. He and his wife
go about their business,
sleeping peacefully at night.

INTERLUDE FOR A SOLITARY FLUTE

What is the age of the couple
of whom there is only one left?
She spoke only a little French,
he spoke a lot.
She was very fond of fruit
and ate it every day.
He liked meat
and that was that.
They both loved
that famous line of
Chinese poetry.
The ambulance stopped
at the wrong house,
losing time.
Here is their house
surrounded by violet clover

and flashing lights.
Who is that weeping,
which one is that,
husband or wife?
Such a high, solitary,
silver note . . .

MUGUET DES BOIS

I was an unopened
action figure
hidden inside
an egg inside
an ovary.
The next thing
I knew I was
on the couch
reading
Madame Bovary.
And when I finished
I could not move.
I took to bed with
Anna Karenina
and a great zoom of
sadness on top of me.
The paper came
from trees,

I pressed flowers
between the pages
and had a forest
where I could talk
and not be overheard.
And still I could
not walk.

DISPIRITED WHILE PACKING MY BOOKS AWAY ONE SUMMER MORNING, I UTILIZE PHRASES FROM ONE THAT WAS DESTINED FOR FODDER

By the Ming there were well over
A thousand theorists of poetry.
Some believed poems "look up into
Vast space and continue nothing"
(I saw a field full of empty snow).
Others that poems were like
"A lotus in first sunlight."
Lotus after lotus
Into the dark boxes.
I looked up from packing,
And continued packing.

THE DEATH OF ATAHUALPA AT THE HANDS OF PIZARRO'S MEN

He couldn't read
so when they handed him The Book
he threw it on the ground
like a useless, heavy thing
and they killed him then and there
making sure that he was dead

Perhaps every death
is as simple as that

A simple sad mistake
under the azure sky
where birds with gold feelings
watch what is happening below
and form a circle overhead

It may be our heads
are filled with feathers
from the stuff
we don't know

SINGULAR DREAM

I was born in Speckled Eggs Garden.
I will die on Broken Egg Farm.
I'm hopping between them now,
I consider everything
to be friendly
and nothing dubbed.
I am a chick with legs
and yellow hair.
O Lord Almighty, creator of
all things beautiful and sick,
who prefers another life on top of this,
who are you to judge?
When Adam and Eve vanished
solemnly into the dark,
shrouding themselves in the forest,
I was timid and nibbling and
stayed behind, betrayed only
by the plucking of my beak

upon the ground you so graciously
provided (thanks).
I did noth with the best,
I am nothing now, do ye
noth with me or not?
Hear me now before I break
O Lord of the Margent,
Lord of noth and straw and all things
sent far, cheerio, sincerely,
I sleep on one leg too!

PATIENCE

I've seen her walking the streets
in her greatcoat, head down,
hair blown back. I've seen the dogs
straining at leashes
in search of her. Her perfume
is death, a black silhouette.
In May, she straightens up,
shortcuts through the hotel
lobby, losing her scarf
which was strangling her.
And then I lost her,
but wait—
Summer, my god here she comes,
floating on air—
I can only imagine what
she's been through,
reeking like that
of gardenia.

LIGHTLY, VERY LIGHTLY

It was raining.
I could hear the rain
taking the pins out of her mouth.
Soft rain became hard rain
so that hard things became soft things.
The wet leaves under the trees
became heavy as diapers,
the book left open
on the grass
could finally sink in her bath
without a word,
the way, after a hard day,
I rest my head on the edge
of the claw-foot tub and
my mouth falls open, empty
at last.
Actually I saw that in a painting
when I ducked into a gallery

because it was raining.
It is always raining somewhere,
somewhere the wells are filling
from above and from below.
Somewhere someone is sleeping,
somewhere the lady of the house
puts the alarm clock in a drawer
where she cannot hear it
then tells the children to be quiet
and stands there listening
to its tick.

INGLENOOK

I live in the museum of
everyday life,
where the thimble is hidden
anew every week and often
takes ten days to find.
Once it was simply lying
(laying?) on the floor
and I missed it,
looking inside my mouth.
A grease fire in the inglenook!
That took a lot of soda!
Free admission, but guests
are required to facewash
before entering and
toothclean before leaving.
Open daily, the doorknobs
are covered with curated
fingerprints, and pass
on the latest news.

SUPER BOWL

Who won? I said.
The game's tomorrow, he said.
And I became the snail I always was,
crossing the field in my helmet.
But I'd given it my all,
while the plane arced on its way
to a landing, when I overheard
the woman behind us say
I was gathering wildflowers to make a wreath
to lay on my mother's grave when my son
fell off a mountain in Italy
and I felt such joy over the unknown
outcome of her words
I was not ashamed,
for I can feign interest
in the world, just as she
in that great green meadow
must have.

JEWELWEED

Mother and daughter
spend the summer
popping jewelweed pods.
A sensitive plant, its pods
explode at the slightest touch.
A train passes on the other side
of the river. Little girls
in the water frantically wave
their teenage dolls, while
a woman on a towel rolls over,
while hope is in a napkin
buried in the earth like salt.
Mother and daughter touch
another pod and the lifeguard's
whistle warns the boys
not to jump from the bridge.
A single cattail holds more energy
than a ton of coal.
And at night the stars ask the day
if things aren't other than they seem.

THE UNFURL

I can't say—some say
the acid green, some say
the sticky yellowness of spring
others the tense lime of it
you know, the color
after hours of slumber, after being vexed
living buds turn out to be leaves
but it only happens in a soft rain
no more than a couple days, a week
at most—
Mozart! wafting from tree to tree
trying to say something with his hands
the leaves so helpless and small
one bird calls to another bird
something friendly and innocuous
kid-chat then seriouser and seriouser
until it sounds like they're in love
the leaves unfurl a little more

a little more after that
until they are whole creatures
capable of touching
who can make it through the night
animals are born now
the skeletal covered by fur
and flesh and hair and leaves
in this way we go on
joining the dead

SEQUOIA

I keep some moss in a bowl
tiny unreal deer there
looking out over the hills
for some water

at the black glass lake
alone at the edge
I stand shaking myself out
didn't think to bring a towel

THE NOTE

The little note
You left by the green soap
After the room was empty
I took it

Go to Greenland
Go straight to the boat
Do not even stop to get coffee

When you see the icebergs
Say hi

Melting they told me
Everything is going to be fine

SPECIAL DELIVERY

Overnight the ground
seems not to have moved,
the sun that was ablood
when it went to bed
has taken a shower,
the white cat on top of the fence
will not say where he slept
and on the birdbath
sits the brown bird
who writes me a letter
each morning
from someone I have not
heard from in years.
Verily, verily
the news is good.

A NEW DAWN

It became clearer and clearer.
Finally it was perfectly clear
and then it resembled Napoleon's funeral,
the most purple and gold Paris
had ever seen, bees and lilies
embroidered on every available inch.
Purple is the color of talking about the past
and the future as if they were the same thing.
Gold is the color of mirth and shambles.
You loved and were loved
said the bee to the lily
before buzzing off.
And the sun spoke:
I will drag you along
but the coffin you carry
must be empty.

NIXIE

It began with a phone number.
Then a grocery list.
A postcard to a dead friend
and then a long letter
in the green hell of a long summer.
With queer little geometrical figures
in the margins.
Then winter came with the monstrosity
of a true artist, its snow didn't know
whether to play Bach or Beethoven,
its light in a light all its own.
I called and called. I went shopping
but the black diamonds downtown
were not on sale, so I am writing
to tell you the ring you wanted
will have to wait, we are telling
stories around the brazier, it is
warm near the tripod and snug,

the hour makes a soft music
all its own, I wish more than anything
you were here beside us, and not
under the maple in Mr. Morioka's garden.
I used to think everything had meaning—
and it does.

LITTLE TRAVEL BOOK

The garage door slowly opens.
A black car rolls out, backwards.
Who knows where it's headed?
This is sad, like Stonehenge in the rain.
The car turns north and drives away.
In a thousand years,
will we ever know its destination?
The purpose of its driver?
Imagine a line of beetles
glued in a cigarette case.
This car is one of them.
Alone, it doesn't mean much,
but in a line the ancient sight
still has the power to inspire us.
If only the car would break down,
we could pinpoint it, we could circle it
on our maps, and other insufferable details
without which life would be unbearable,

no longer recognizable,

simply a stupendous mystery

and a cloud of smoke at that.

This much we know: They circled Walter

after the accident. He was crying as

they washed his feet, which were

some distance from his body.

GRANDMA MOSES

Real snow glitters,
so add glitter to the paint
when painting snow.
When the barn burns
study a cat's tongue
for the shape of the flames
for flames lick the air,
there is no end to their
convulsive tenderness.
Then coat them in
red and orange feathers.
Annamoses is the state
of being oneself.
In this state there is a village
where children do nothing
but play. And there is hay,
piles and piles of hay.
You can stay.

You can bury yourself
in the hay.
Hooray! Hooray!
It's Annamoses Day!
Eating beets
with a pitchfork
is ok.

THE HEART OF PRINCESS OSRA

I want to slow down and reflect,
like the top waters of a lake
or the heart of Princess Osra
who had nine suitors at one time.
I want to thank my clothes for
protecting my body. I want to
fold them properly—I want
the energy that flows from my hands
to engulf the world.
Upon reflection, this is not
possible. Upon reflection
it is I who am pummeled by
the world, that vast massage
machine, and so is the sheen
of many waters, and Princess Osra
surely too was pummeled by the world,
which is so full of hands and clothes.
The same is true, I think, for babies.

LILLIAN

Jesus was in way over his head.
That's why he wore a halo.
That's why he made her a star (though
no one could have played a better he than she)
in *Way Down East*, *Broken Blossoms*,
Orphans of the Storm, and *Hearts of the World*.
But the trouble with the spirit of art is
if I think of Lillian I forget Braque—reformed,
destroyed, resuscitated—and I forget Li Ho,
who rode a donkey, stuffing his knapsack
with scraps of writing to shuffle later into
discontinuous poems, and I forget Morandi,
who lived in his mother's apartment and painted
bottles far into the night. When I look into
Lillian's eyes I forget everything else,
which is what love is, so Jesus forgot the few
nails in his wrists and Braque was able to paint
him that way, as a woman holding a mandolin,
and Morandi threw what looks like a stone
into one of his bottles, thus painting
the secret of life exposed.

WINTERSAULT

Snowflakes would be more gladsome
but when warmship isn't there
they get mummed down to a hair
Mind you the nay-word has some mastery over us
I cried once when it stopped snowing
A flake looked at me so queer
The queer look of a flake is a sneer
It leaves things ice for a year
I be marvelous barbarous gladsome
when the nay-word be lyin' in the wood
breathin' regular and Christmas bells
far off, but here comes the cold morn
who wants a jagged piece of nay in my neck
when I want to be left floatin' in a warm pool
in sum where I belong

DESTINATION

Called by a friend
to come to her rental
to see from a window
someone breaking into the sea

Would I see a man
peeing into the sea
cuz the nightingale is asleep
and he feels like rubble?

Would I see a woman
throwing a stone into the sea,
sending an urgent message
to her past?

Would I see children
singing by the sea
like gilly glowers
updating the air?

Would I see the tears
of their grandparents
flowing toward the sea
but never making it?

So much is
beautifully situated to meet a real need

Our bathing suits cling to our bodies
as we come out of the sea

At the restaurant we pass
the salt over the body of the fish

and speak in half-sentences
each one somehow partly many

HAPPY BIRTHDAY

This day
a wild forest,
being at home

This day
trees meet perhaps
and rejoice

This day
announcing
the importance of confetti

This day
we take up the hem
of our sorrow

This day
wherein we love one another more than ever
but lose the desire to prove it

This day
once upon a time and maybe
nowadays who knows

This day
knows exactly where we are
and how much time is left

This day
spake to the Great Turk
then whispered to us

This day
crosses the river of tenderness
like a berry to the rescue

This day
was wet on top and happy
like a cupcake

This day
the mystic drama of a clumsy hare
is filmed in gold

This day
the meanders of an insouciant cow
end in a field of daisies

This day
the elves' disquisition is dedicated to us,
the wishbone sails our way

This day
the most passionate form of repair
and resurrection, a button found in the ocean

This day
the atom remembers to make friends on earth
a billion maybe two

This day
shall I ejaculate?

This day
O beautiful thou art
in spite of thy Great Naughtiness

This day
of trembling joy, I know not whether
you can fit it into your laws

This day
it did happen and it happened
exactly the way we remembered it

Exactly

To be alone in a dead world
breathing forever did not happen on
this day

(sing again)

ORIGIN MYTH

It was midnight
anxious friends
Life continually
circled in cold
inaccessible serenity
around unhappy Earth
Then all at once
swallowed it
Ever after
the humming
of bees at noon
could be heard
Even as you swam
across the bottom
of your dark
suburban pool

THE CAKE

Where would you like to be?
A little closer to the window, please.
And the soul of my mother spake, saying
You should have spoken sooner.
I heard my father's soul say
You should have listened to me,
Then I was wheeled to the window.
I saw the mist over the grass
Of all words, my mistakes carefully
Wrapped in a blanket and sung to.
On the corner sat a bakery.
A cake sat in the window,
Waiting for the world to wake up.

A MORNING PERSON

What a beautiful day for a wedding!
It was raining when we buried my mum,
she loved lilacs and here they are,
the lilac lilacs like pendulous
large breasts dripping with dew,
I am enjoying them alone with my
mug of coffee, which I also enjoy
with the intensity of a remark
made in a surgical theater.
Soon I will vacuum the day,
not a speck of it will remain,
I will suck it up like a bee
at the tit, making a hoopla.
But now it is quiet, hardly anyone
is dressed, not a doggie is walking.
I think flowers enjoy their solitude
in the early dawn before the buzz begins.
I think sprinklers annoy them.
I hear one coming on.
I hate my poems.

VOW OF EXTINCTION

From this day forward all plants
except the lemon tree
will be banished from my poems

From this day forward I am wedded to the sky

All clouds shall be banished
and my memory of them vanish
like memory itself

Not even a lime shall sneak in

Animals shall exit my poems
including those that cross the sky
in herds or as stragglers

Without plants, without animals
people cannot survive in my poems

so they too shall be sent,
those with shoes and those without
in a long line leaving

Leaving myself under the lemon tree
wedded to the sky
that is light then dark then light

Candles are forbidden

I will feel the terrible weight of twilight
as it falls over the land like a despondent minx,
words I might formerly have used for a squirrel

From this cretinous proposition
I shall write my poems
and try to reach those
who no longer exist

They are not in this poem or any other

From this day forward
I eat lemons in my park

Their complete similarity to me
can now be distinguished

To speak of my promise,
my offering to the sky,
puts a sprig in my mouth

Would this not then be my entry into society?

HOW WE MET

I very much dislike being at a buffet

The first time I saw
the little man in the radish swing
swinging out over the vegetable tray
was himself a radish,
I was happy

I would be happiest if there were
a whole village of radish people,
as many radish people
as there are buffet people
I hope for each radish person
a "sister person" in the room

I am half radish myself

Some say the best thing you can do
is carry a pair of little scissors,

snip small pieces of the world
and take them home with you

These scissors have cut hair
These scissors have cut nails
From these scissors come my fragments

You can cut a rose from a radish
or little people who are happy swinging
in a room of bigger people, the excited throng
cut from cloth

At the banquet I stood next to him
When I pushed the swing he smiled at me
Fast friends are the best
It is good to have a bunch of them

We each chose a piece of
preposterous melon and
for the sake of a little quiet
removed the seeds

You see?
From radishes come joy

ERRAND

To find things out—
that is the great adventure!
To find out the writing on the birthday cake
was toothpaste.
To find out Musical Chairs
was for real.
Find out Lord made the world
then threw the leftover rocks
in a pile and left.
Nettles growing nearby
spliced themselves into
days—find it out!
Checkless griff. Bitter love.
Modern hell. Bloody tears.
Beneath an ordinary glance
dwells an explosive.
Go to market.
Find all this out,

find everything out.
Even if your last day is
incomplete, even if something up there
thinks you are marzipan,
keep finding out—
for the stork who dropped us off
in the wilderness returns,
but with a bigger maw this time
so he can accommodate us
and all that we have found out
even if the terriblest part
is so condensed
we bear a resemblance
to the night sky.

THE BUTTER FESTIVAL

You can have all the other sadnesses:
the yellow leaf on the burnt path,
the silverware hopelessly scratched,
the evening news and the morning news,
the funeral, the rotgut, the crappy
tag sale, the dead fish seasoning the
shore, the memorial, the wake, the Ono
no Komachi poems, all of April
1998, the lunar new year murder,
English as she is spoke, and
the attempt to resist an inevitability
that you yourself created.
The fourteenth way of looking at
a blackbird is *mine*,
and a couple of other sad experiences
rolled into a ball of pie dough
as an object lesson in fragility
for the butter festival.

30 MARCH

The daffodils came out
with trumpets, announcing
they would start today
for the Holy Grail.
Poor things! Poor things!
If it is to be,
I plan to watch.
Barefoot shivering creatures
at the foot of the
Great Norwegian Spruce.

HALLOWEEN

The corpse had a motion detector
and when you approached it
it sat up and stretched out its arms
its eyes rolled back to white
and then the most peculiar thing—
it turned its head around,
all the way around, 360,
then said something stupid.
It wasn't gross or funny
in no way frightening
rather sweetly sad especially
when that head turned round
and reminded me of my mother
and at the thought of my mother
there was a corpse in *me*,
it sat up and stretched out its arms
rolled those eyeballs back
turned its head all the way around

then said something stupid
like *old long since mum.*
If only I'd sung the whole song.
Should old acquaintance be forgot,
and never brought to mind?

BOUTONNIERE

Standing alone after the harvest
and what is the point of dreams?

At some age,
the world begins to drift away

The world is changed
as you came here

The people you really like
a lot will disappear

How many years of opacity
have led (like a barnyard dance)
to this transparent moment?

Over the course of a life
why have I nowhere commented
on what steps were easy?

1) loving you—
2) watching wild doings among the animals—
3) standing with friends looking at sky—

easier than making a boutonniere out of old sheets!
easier than hanging a new shower curtain!
easier than my sudden life-changing switcheroo!
easier than being Brueghel's little brother . . .

GENESIS

Oh, I said, this is going to be.
And it was.
Oh, I said, this will never happen.
But it did.
And a purple fog descended upon the land.
The roots of trees curled up.
The world was divided into two countries.
Every photograph taken in the first was of people.
Every photograph taken in the second showed none.
All of the girl children were named And.
All of the boy children named Then.

THE LEAVES

Dearly beloved, we are gathered
here together today to look into
the face of the river.
One of us has stayed at home
to rake the leaves,
gathering those poor tears
shed for the rest of us.
If there is one among you
who sees in the face of the river
your own, please step forward
and identify the source of your
wealth. If not, can you give us
a thumbnail sketch
of the important philosophers
in Golden Greece?

An old cedar stood by,
simply thankful she existed.

And a young fox, who had
neither dreams nor feelings
in this French.
And the one at a distance
raking the leaves did not
think of them as tears,
but as simple toil, conducted
without compromise.
In the sweet fresh morning
how good it was to be alone
with potato parings filling
his mind. To whom should he speak?
There was no one but the leaves
and the leaves did not feel
he had anything worth saying.

ACKNOWLEDGMENTS

Some of these poems first appeared in *Bennington Review*, *Big Big Wednesday*, *Catamaran Literary Review*, *Columbia Poetry Review*, *Connotation Press*, *Denver Quarterly*, *F(r)iction*, *Granta*, *jubilat*, *Jung Journal*, *Kenyon Review*, *Los Angeles Review of Books*, *Mal* (London), *Mississippi Review*, *Music & Literature*, *The New Yorker*, *Plume*, *Poetry*, *The Poetry Review* (London), *Roads Taken: Contemporary Vermont Poetry*, *Salt Hill*, *The Sewanee Review*, *Sonora Review*, *Tuesday; An Art Project*, *Turbine* (New Zealand), and *The Volta*.

"I Cannot Be Quiet an Hour" was originally published online for the Academy of American Poets Poem-a-Day feature

"A Late Dense Work" quotes the artist Stuart Williams

"Tuna and a Play" is for Jody Gladding

"Attention!" is for David Hinton

"The Note" is for Jean Valentine

"How We Met" (a true story) is in memory of Tomaž Šalamun

A deep bow to Marian MacDowell

Now take this flea—
He simply cannot jump
And I love him for it.

ISSA